MINDFULNESS

in your pocket

ANNA BARNES

MINDFULNESS IN YOUR POCKET

This edition copyright © Summersdale Publishers Ltd, 2021
First published in 2016 as *How to Be Mindful*

Design by Luci Ward

Research by Katherine Bassford

Illustrations © Shutterstock.com

An Hachette UK Company
www.hachette.co.uk

Vie Books, an imprint of Summersdale Publishers Ltd
Part of Octopus Publishing Group Limited
Carmelite House
50 Victoria Embankment
LONDON
EC4Y 0DZ
UK

www.summersdale.com

Printed and bound in China

ISBN: 978-1-78783-661-7

Substantial discounts on bulk quantities of Summersdale books are available to corporations, professional associations and other organizations. For details contact general enquiries: telephone: +44 (0) 1243 771107 or email: enquiries@summersdale.com.

CONTENTS

INTRODUCTION

Mindfulness is about focusing on the magic of the present moment. Rather than fretting about the past or worrying about the future, the aim is to experience life as it unfolds moment by moment. This simple practice is immensely powerful. As we rush through our lives, mindfulness encourages us to stop constantly striving for something new or better and to embrace acceptance and gratitude. This allows us to tap into the joy and wonder in our lives, and to listen to the wisdom of our hearts. This book will show you how to experience small but beautiful moments of mindfulness every day and so guide you along the path to finding more peace and contentment in your life.

A LITTLE BIT
OF MINDFULNESS
EVERY DAY

A NEW DAY BEGINS.

On waking in the morning, rather than springing out of bed to start your busy day, spend a few moments becoming aware of your surroundings. Listen to the sounds around you and notice what thoughts are in your mind. Sit up straight, place your feet on the floor, and tune in to your body. Focus on your breathing and allow your stomach to rise and fall. Imagine that you are breathing in the morning light. Visualize each breath flooding your body with golden light from the rising sun. Feel energized, ready for the day ahead.

What a benediction
is this fragrance of
the early morning!

Sarah Smiley

LET YOUR STRESSES FLOAT AWAY

Visualization can be a powerful meditation tool. If you are feeling anxious, visualize a hot air balloon and imagine that you are putting all your stress and negativity into the balloon. Then watch it gently float away into the distance, taking your worries and concerns with it.

START SMALL

Mindfulness is not something you achieve overnight; it is a habit which is developed gradually over time. The best approach is to take baby steps. Start by picking one or two opportunities to treat with a mindful attitude every day. You might decide to be mindful every time you brush your teeth, walk to the car, open a door or make a cup of tea, for example. Whichever action you choose, make sure you give your whole attention to it. When you open a door, watch your hand grasp the doorknob, feel the weight of the door as you pull it open, and hear the sounds of whatever is on the other side of the doorway... If you do this every time you open a door, you will be amazed at how automatic this process becomes. This simple ritual will allow mindfulness to establish a foothold in your life. All you need to do is take baby steps and commit to being mindful for a few seconds several times a day.

LEARN THE RIGHT TECHNIQUE

You can learn mindfulness in numerous ways to suit your preferences and budget. If you're an auditory learner, you could buy a mindfulness CD or podcast to guide you into a meditative state. If you prefer to learn directly from a teacher, consider signing up to a local introductory class or investing in some one-to-one tuition. Many yoga courses and retreats also include mindfulness meditation as part of the curriculum. Learning in a group has the benefit of a strong atmosphere of community and friendship, but if you prefer to learn in the privacy of your own home, try taking an online course such as the one at www.bemindful.co.uk.

INSTRUCTION FOR LIFE:

PAY ATTENTION.

Whatever the present
moment contains, accept it
as if you had chosen it.

Eckhart Tolle

USE VISUAL CUES

Being mindful is not difficult to do – it's the remembering that's the key! Place inspiring pictures and notes around your home to remind you and your family to "be mindful", "pause" and "take a breath". These visual triggers can be all you need to snap you back to the present moment.

I CAN
&
I WILL

THINGS
TO BE
GRATEFUL
FOR

Start a daily gratitude journal. List all the positive things in your life – from the small things that make you smile, such as the view from your window, to the bigger things, such as your health or your family. At night, list three things you were grateful for during the day and you'll soon start focusing naturally on the positives.

EVERYDAY
MINDFULNESS

Many of us go through our daily
routines on automatic pilot, barely
noticing what we are doing. An easy
way to focus your attention on the
present moment is to focus on simple
tasks. For instance, make your bed
with 100 per cent focus and attention
each morning so you create a calm
transition from bedroom and sleep
to the outside world and the rest of
your day. Similarly, when cleaning
your teeth or brushing your hair,
notice every sensory detail. You
might also find it useful to sit quietly
for a few minutes in the morning
so that you can calmly contemplate
the day ahead, instead of rushing
straight into your day's activities.

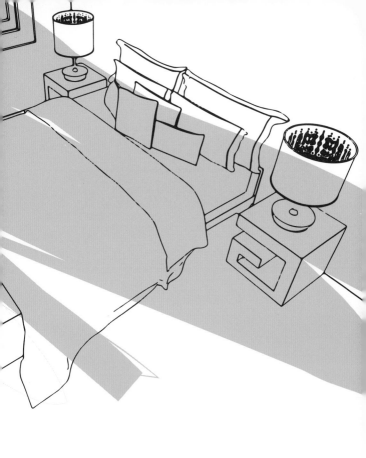

DIGITAL DETOX

The non-stop stream of information we receive from mobiles, computers and TVs can be overwhelming. It's a good idea to give our mental "inbox" a break from time to time. Turn off your devices, hide all gadgets and give yourself some time off from the endless technological invasion in your life.

The greatest step
towards a life of
simplicity is to
learn to let go.

Steve Maraboli

SEE
THE GOOD
EVERYWHERE.

FORGIVE AND FORGET

Open your heart and soul to forgiveness, both for yourself and others. Holding on to resentment or anger only fuels other negative emotions. Be open to healing and love.

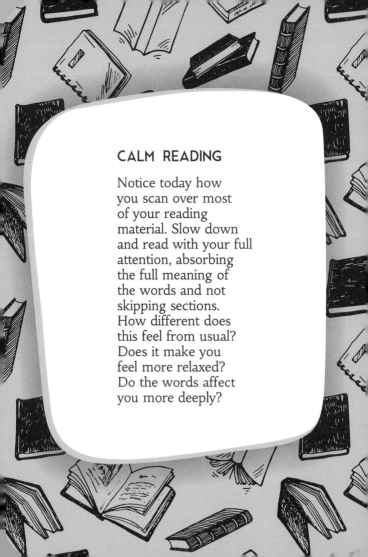

CALM READING

Notice today how
you scan over most
of your reading
material. Slow down
and read with your full
attention, absorbing
the full meaning of
the words and not
skipping sections.
How different does
this feel from usual?
Does it make you
feel more relaxed?
Do the words affect
you more deeply?

Happiness is a Journey, not a Destination.

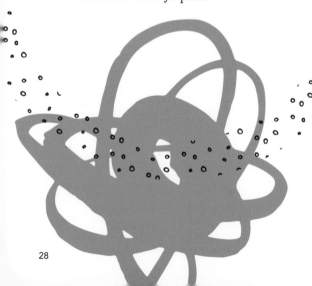

BREATHE INTO TENSION

If you encounter a difficult situation today, notice which parts of your body feel tense, then breathe into the area to help you relax. Remind yourself that challenging moments always pass.

The greatest weapon against
stress is our ability to choose
one thought over another.

William James

THE ORDINARY CAN BE

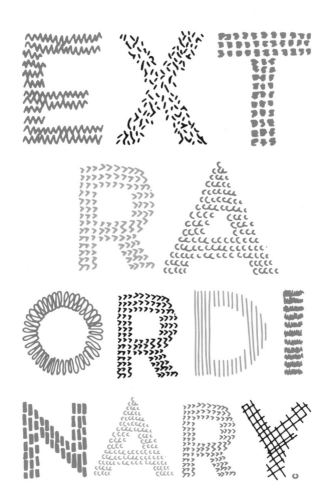

EXTRAORDINARY.

31

Mindfulness
is seeing
things with
fresh eyes.

ORDINARY INTO
EXTRAORDINARY

Take a daily routine activity,
such as cleaning your teeth,
and be curious and alert about
yourself, noticing every sensory
detail. Pay attention to the
contours of your mouth and
the sensation of the brush
against each tooth. Notice
if you're thinking ahead
to what you're doing next
and if so, gently bring your
attention back to the present.

STAND FIRM, LIKE A TREE

A great way to ground yourself when you're in the midst of turmoil, is to take some deep breaths and visualize roots growing from your feet into the ground. Stand firm like a tree, while the chaos around you blows through your branches and disappears on the breeze.

In the midst of movement and chaos, keep stillness inside of you.

Deepak Chopra

The most important
thing about
being mindful

is remembering to be mindful.

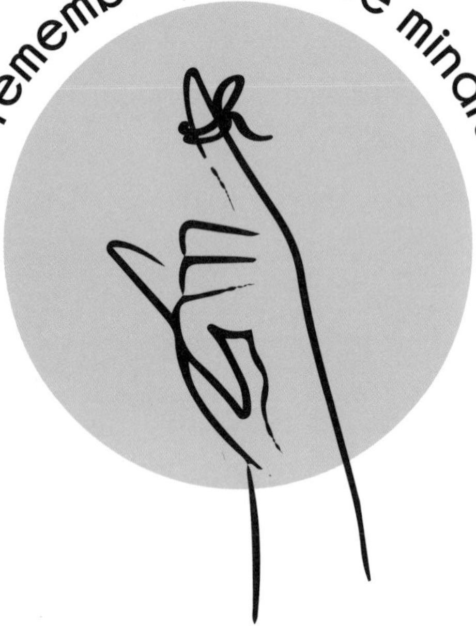

MAKE MORE MEMORIES

Don't take things for granted. Everyday moments, when experienced fully, can become lifelong memories – from savouring the first freshly picked strawberries of the season or the blackbird's song outside your window to holding a new-born child.

Whenever you arrive
somewhere, give yourself
a moment to "check in".
Become aware of how your
body is feeling – especially
any aches and tensions. Take
note of what emotions you
are carrying. Acknowledge all
of this, taking no more than a
minute, and you will be centred
and present, ready to move on.

An awake heart
is like a sky that
pours light.

Hāfez

MAKE
TODAY
A
"NO RUSH"
DAY.

When you're in a rush – dashing around the supermarket or taking the dog for a quick walk – bring your awareness to your feet. Slow down slightly and feel your feet connect you to the ground. This will help you to gain a sense of equilibrium and balance.

DON'T JUMP TO CONCLUSIONS

There is great truth in the familiar saying, "Don't judge a book by its cover." We often prejudge people by their appearance or the sound of their voice. Being mindful means seeing everything in the present moment, without leaping to unfounded conclusions.

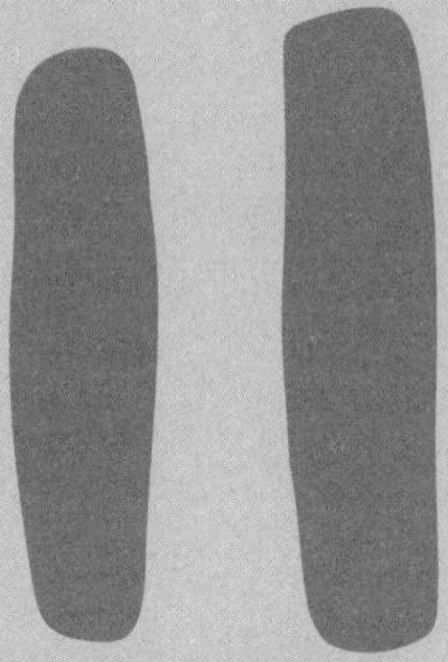

||

PAUSE

**IT'S WHAT
GIVES YOU
YOUR POWER.**

YOU ALWAYS HAVE A CHOICE
IN HOW TO RESPOND.

CHOOSE YOUR REACTION

Strong emotions, such as anger, hurt or fear, can erupt very quickly. But there's usually a split second in which you can pause before you react. When you feel something inside you being triggered, become mindful of your breath. Notice the sensations in your body. Realize you have a choice about what you do next before you react.

PRACTISE MINDFUL LISTENING

We often find that when we listen
to others we are concentrating on
what to say next, filling up our minds
with our own opinions or even
speaking out of turn. Try listening
with mindfulness – hear the person
without judgement or the need
to immediately express a view. Be
aware that the word "listen" can be
shuffled around to spell "silent".

BREATHE INTO YOUR BELLY

Take a moment to "belly breathe" for a greater flow of oxygen and instant calm. Breathe in deeply, allowing your stomach to rise outwards. On the out-breath, allow your stomach to fall back.

LET
GO OF
THE

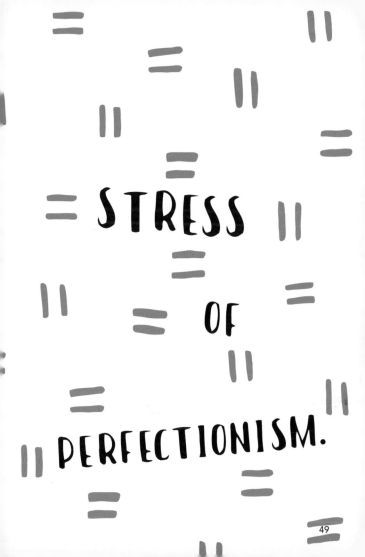

STRESS OF PERFECTIONISM.

CONNECT WITH PEOPLE

Take time out to sit on a bench or a
window seat in a cafe and watch people
go by. Don't read, talk or catch up on
social media – just people-watch. Feel
connected to everyone and watch them
with an open mind and compassion.

The more we notice
things to appreciate,
the more they
seem to grow.

STICK WITH IT

Developing a daily mindfulness
practice takes patience and
determination. It can be hard work
to keep pulling your mind back
to the present moment. There
will be challenges and obstacles to
overcome, not least the fact that
the benefits of mindfulness may
be quite subtle at first. There may
be times when you want to throw
in the towel, but be determined. If
you persevere, you will learn from
obstacles and overcome them. Your
ability will improve and the benefits
will start to become more obvious.
You will start to feel more present,
peaceful and alive. Whenever you
feel your patience wavering, remind
yourself that mindfulness works
like a muscle – the more you
exercise it, the stronger it gets.

THE POWER OF THE MIND

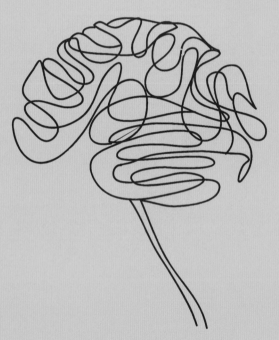

The mind… can be compared
to the sky, covered by
layers of cloud which
hide its true nature.

Kalu Rinpoche

YOU ARE NOT
YOUR THOUGHTS

Do your thoughts overwhelm and confuse you?
Do you wish your mind had an "off" button?
Much of our suffering stems from the fact that
we think our thoughts are the core of our being.
We identify with our thoughts and allow them to
dictate how we feel. As our thoughts are often
"noisy", negative and chaotic, it's no wonder we
struggle. The solution lies not in trying to get
rid of our thoughts altogether but in stopping
our habit of identifying with them. Simply
observe your thoughts without judgement and
let them go. You do not have to be a slave to
your thoughts and feelings. What gives them
fuel and makes them real is the attention
you bring to them. Take away that attention,
and that thought or feeling ceases to exist!

NOTICE WHAT DISTRACTS YOU

We each have unique tendencies or thoughts that pull us away from the present moment. Start paying attention to your thoughts and jot down the types of thoughts that distract you most often. Do you have a tendency to dwell on the past or the future? Are you consumed with thoughts of guilt, fear, regret or worry? Do you ruminate on achieving perfection or success, wealth and recognition? Writing these tendencies down can help you become more mindful about what is going on in your head when you stray from the present moment. This insight can lead you to mindfulness.

LISTEN TO YOUR HEART AND TRUST YOUR INSTINCTS.

STOP ASSUMING
THE WORST

If your mind is racing and you are consumed with worry, are you scaring yourself with "what-ifs"? What-ifs and imagined scenarios may seem incredibly real but they are a figment of our imagination. A large proportion of the things we imagine never actually happen. Let's say you take your cat to the vets because he has stopped eating and you spend the day before the appointment worrying that the vet will discover a terrible disease. In reality, the vet finds a splinter in your cat's gum and removes it, solving the problem. Yet you spent the previous day gripped with anxiety. If worrying is controlling your life, it's time to take control. The second you realize you are dwelling on a worst-case scenario, bring yourself back to the present. Remind yourself that you are not a fortune teller! Worrying serves no purpose other than to make you feel anxious. Focus on the facts of a situation and on what is (rather than what-ifs!).

Accept people for
who they are,

including yourself!

FORGIVE YOURSELF

Self-compassion is essential when learning mindfulness. You will not be able to sustain mindfulness 100 per cent of the time. You may be "too busy" to practise or forget to practise altogether. You may be unable to stop your mind from wandering, or you may find yourself thinking about being mindful rather than practising being mindful! The ability to forgive yourself at these times is crucial. Self-compassion will enable you to pick yourself up, dust yourself off and try again. If you beat yourself up every time you falter, you will be far less likely to stick to the kind of regular practice which will impact on your health and happiness.

THERE IS NO DESTINATION!

When we embark on a new project, we normally have a goal or destination in mind. The beauty of mindfulness is that it is a process; there is no end destination. You cannot exist outside of the present moment. Life is what is happening to you right now. So the only goal when practising mindfulness is to be fully present. It can be helpful to remind yourself of this on a regular basis. You might like to write the following mantra on a piece of paper and put it somewhere where you can see it every day: There is nowhere more important for you to be than right here, right now.

WAYS TO INVITE
MINDFULNESS
INTO YOUR LIFE

COME
HOME
TO THE
PRESENT.

GIVE IN TO YOUR CREATIVE URGE

Try something creative –
draw or paint a picture,
write a story about your
childhood or play a piece
of music. Don't worry
about the quality of what
you're producing, and
don't hold back – the
most important thing
is to immerse yourself
in the joy of creating!

IMMERSE
YOURSELF
IN MUSIC

Listening to music can be a great mindfulness exercise. Choose music that is soothing: instrumental or classical are good choices. Begin by sitting with a comfortable, upright posture. Choose a space where you can minimize any outer distractions and be sure to turn off your phone, computer and television. Spend a few moments breathing fully and completely, immersing yourself in your inhalation and exhalation. As you begin to listen to the music, focus on the sound and vibration of each note. Notice any feelings that the music conjures up for you and any sensations that occur in your body as you listen. If other thoughts creep into your head, gently bring your attention back to the music. Afterwards, notice how much calmer you feel.

Plan a mindful weekend without clocks or watches. Listen to your body instead – you choose when to get up, when to eat, what tasks you feel like doing and the length of time you spend on them.

We have only now, only
this single eternal moment
opening and unfolding
before us, day and night.

Jack Kornfield

SAVOUR HOUSEWORK

Here's a great way to turn housework from a chore into an enjoyable activity: be completely present as you wash, scrub, dust and hoover – and do it without rushing. Savour every sensory detail. While washing up for example, notice every rainbow bubble, the warm water and the shining dishes. Feel a sense of satisfaction at a small job well done.

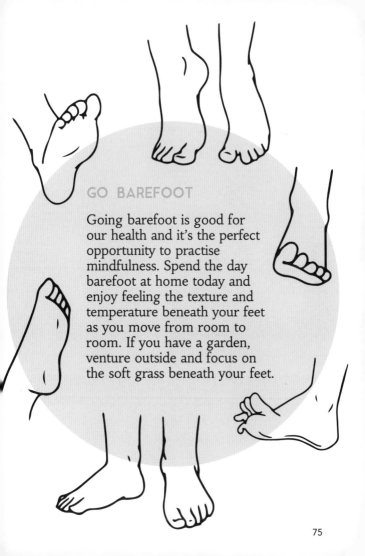

GO BAREFOOT

Going barefoot is good for our health and it's the perfect opportunity to practise mindfulness. Spend the day barefoot at home today and enjoy feeling the texture and temperature beneath your feet as you move from room to room. If you have a garden, venture outside and focus on the soft grass beneath your feet.

BE AWAKE TO NEW EXPERIENCES

When travelling to a new place, it is easy to get distracted by taking photographs and buying souvenirs. Make sure you get the most out of the experience by bringing your presence and full attention to all that you experience. Savour the sights, sounds and smells of your new location.

LOOK FOR THINGS TO BE THANKFUL FOR.

TRY SOMETHING NEW

You are instinctively being mindful whenever your brain is engaged in something unfamiliar. So make it your goal to try new things from time to time, whether that's learning a musical instrument or going to an art class. If you feel anxiety, fear or resistance when facing a new activity, mindfully notice that you are experiencing fear of the unknown. Be kind to yourself. Instead of shutting down or holding back, simply switch to an activity you find less scary to begin with. Whether it's skydiving or a salsa class, by slowly building confidence you can enjoy new hobbies and experience more moments of mindfulness.

Put your ear down close to
your soul and listen hard.

Anne Sexton

PAUSE BEFORE
ANSWERING THE PHONE

Allow the telephone
to ring three times
before you reply,
so that you can
become aware of
your breath and
speak from a centred
and calm space.

TAKE ADVANTAGE
OF QUEUES

Turn inconvenient moments
in your day into opportunities
for mindfulness. If you're stuck
in a queue at the supermarket
or in a traffic jam, become
aware of how your body,
posture and thoughts are
affected by the situation.

Life happens.

Let it be.

TAKE A
POWER SHOWER

Transform your shower
or bath by bringing
your full attention to the
experience. Feel the warm
water against your skin
and listen to the sound it
makes. Savour the scent
of the soap and shampoo
and be aware of the
variety of textures beneath
your hands. Imagine that
you are washing yourself
clean of any negativity.

GET DRESSED MINDFULLY

As you get dressed and undressed, slow the process down and observe whether your movements are comfortable and flowing, or hasty and rushed. Notice the textures and fabrics of your clothes and how they feel on your skin. Value the fact that you are able to make the decision over what you wear today.

CONQUER INFORMATION OVERLOAD

Reduce your information
consumption. Cancel
subscriptions for magazines
you barely have time to
read and unsubscribe from
catalogues, junk mail and
emails. A cluttered mind
is a stressed mind. Free
up your mind and make
space for the whispers
of your heart and soul.

A MINDFUL
BODY

TUNE IN TO YOUR BODY

The next time you seek out a sugary snack, stop and think about how you are feeling. People often turn to food in an attempt to self-soothe or deal with stressful situations. Recognize that you are looking for something to eat that you think will bring you satisfaction. Sit down and be fully present with this craving. Awareness can often lessen the desire. Maybe you don't need that chocolate biscuit after all!

DO A "BODY SWEEP"

Research shows that our emotions manifest in our body. For example, negative emotions often cause people to tense the muscles in their jaw and around their eyes and mouth. With repeated stress, these muscles can become sore and tight. One of the key ways to balance your mind–body connection is to stop and give yourself a "body sweep".

Sit quietly and systematically scan your body, starting at the top of your head and moving down over your face, the back of your head, your shoulders, arms, hands, torso, hips, legs and feet. As you do this, notice the sensations you feel. Are there any areas of tension, pressure or discomfort? If so, breathe into these areas and allow them to soften and relax. Practising this body sweep on a regular basis can help you become more alert to the messages of your body. The tension you discover might be a "gut feeling" about a choice you're making or a headache may indicate that you need to pay attention to a health issue. By exploring the link between your body and mind, you will start to notice which parts of the body are stimulated or shut down when you experience a particular emotion. "Softening" these areas can help release the tension or emotion stored there.

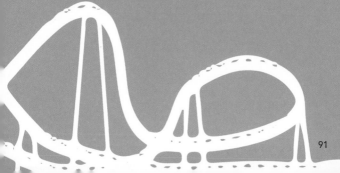

ARE YOU SITTING MINDFULLY?

Bring your awareness to your chair or the ground and become aware of pressures against your body and textures on your skin. Shift your weight to give you greater comfort and notice any areas of tension such as shoulders, lower back or neck.

EVERYTHING HAPPENS FOR A REASON.

BREATHE IN CALM

Wherever you are,
you can incorporate
a calm, breathing
meditation into your
day. Start by becoming
aware of your breath
as it enters and leaves
your nostrils. Breathe
to your own rhythm.
After a few breaths,
focus on breathing
in and breathing
out the feelings you
wish to nurture:

I BREATHE IN CALM. I BREATHE OUT CALM.
I BREATHE IN PEACE. I BREATHE OUT PEACE.
I BREATHE IN LOVE. I BREATHE OUT LOVE.
I BREATHE IN STRENGTH. I BREATHE OUT STRENGTH.
I BREATHE IN HARMONY. I BREATHE OUT HARMONY.

Create as many lines to your meditation as you wish, using words that are meaningful to you and the situation you find yourself in. This meditation is especially helpful if you're about to do something you feel nervous about: a job interview, a meeting with your child's teacher or any other important task.

MINDFUL MOVEMENT

Mindful exercise is about performing physical activity while focusing inward. This allows you to get more in touch with your body. The idea is to let go of distractions and unrelated thoughts, and focus your attention on your breath, movements and sensations. If you do this whilst working out, you will enhance your enjoyment, decrease your chances of injury, and even improve the efficacy of the exercise you're doing. Most importantly, it will help you develop a healthy and loving relationship with your body. Remember, you're aiming for quality, not quantity. Try turning off your TV or iPod and bringing your attention to your breath and your movements while you are jogging, cycling, swimming or lifting weights.

BY BEING
HAPPY IN THIS
MOMENT

YOU ARE
CREATING MORE
HAPPINESS.

As you walk from one place to another, become aware of your posture. Notice if you are rushing ahead, with your shoulders hunched with tension. Straighten your spine and lift your chest and be aware of your connection to the ground as each foot is placed in front of the other. Enjoy being alert and mindful while you walk. Throughout your day, take every opportunity to walk with peace and serenity – when walking to your car, moving from room to room at home or at work, or while out shopping, bring your full presence to the process of walking and you will glide serenely through your day.

You are

exactly

where

you need
to be.

MINDFUL EATING

If you regularly wolf down
your food without really tasting
it, start practising mindfulness
whenever you eat. As you
prepare your food, savour every
culinary aroma. When you sit
down to eat, take a moment to
quietly give thanks for the food
in front of you. As you eat your
meal, focus all your attention on
the tastes, sounds, smells and
sensations you are experiencing,
rather than anything else going
on around you. See if turning
the TV or radio off and eating
in silence makes you appreciate
the food and the feeling of
being full more than usual. Try
placing your fork down in-
between mouthfuls and chewing
each mouthful slowly in order
to relish every taste sensation.

LIKE CLOUDS
IN THE SKY,

EVERYTHING IS IN A CONSTANT PROCESS OF CHANGE.

SPIRITUAL
MINDFULNESS

Meditation practice
isn't about trying
to throw ourselves
away or become
something better. It's
about befriending
who we are already.

Pema Chödrön

SMILE THROUGHOUT YOUR BODY

If you are feeling a little low, try this healing smile meditation. Bring to mind someone or something that makes you smile or laugh – your best friend, your pet or your partner, for example. Soak in the warm feeling you get when you think about them and let the corners of your mouth curl up into a gentle smile. Let this smile gather joy and energy and breathe these good feelings into your heart. On each out-breath, direct this warm, happy glow around your

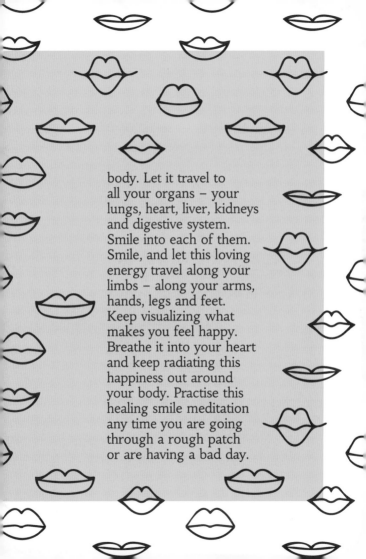

body. Let it travel to all your organs – your lungs, heart, liver, kidneys and digestive system. Smile into each of them. Smile, and let this loving energy travel along your limbs – along your arms, hands, legs and feet. Keep visualizing what makes you feel happy. Breathe it into your heart and keep radiating this happiness out around your body. Practise this healing smile meditation any time you are going through a rough patch or are having a bad day.

It's good to have an
end in mind, but in
the end what counts
is how you travel.

Orna Ross

AFFIRM IT, BELIEVE IT

Affirmations are quiet reminders that you repeat to yourself, either during your meditation or as you go about your day. They can be particularly helpful if you find you are stuck in a negative thought loop. Choose an affirmation that has meaning for you, such as, "Everything that is happening now is happening for my ultimate good" or "I am at peace with the world".

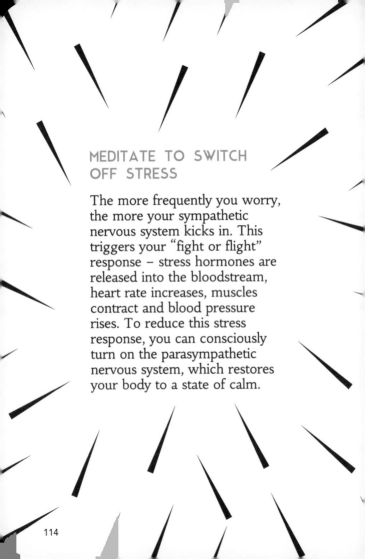

MEDITATE TO SWITCH OFF STRESS

The more frequently you worry, the more your sympathetic nervous system kicks in. This triggers your "fight or flight" response – stress hormones are released into the bloodstream, heart rate increases, muscles contract and blood pressure rises. To reduce this stress response, you can consciously turn on the parasympathetic nervous system, which restores your body to a state of calm.

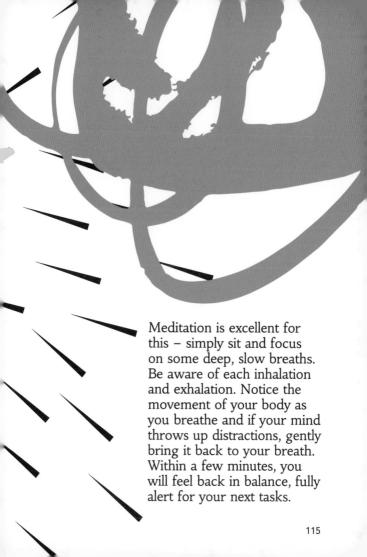

Meditation is excellent for
this – simply sit and focus
on some deep, slow breaths.
Be aware of each inhalation
and exhalation. Notice the
movement of your body as
you breathe and if your mind
throws up distractions, gently
bring it back to your breath.
Within a few minutes, you
will feel back in balance, fully
alert for your next tasks.

LET THOUGHTS
COME AND GO

Many people think that
the goal of meditation is to
achieve a blank mind, with
no thoughts at all, but having
thoughts while you meditate
is perfectly normal. In fact, it's
what's supposed to happen!
Dealing with thoughts is how
mindfulness meditation works.
When you notice that you are
distracted by your thoughts,
gently bring your attention
back to the object of your
meditation. Over time, this
simple practice will change
how you relate to distractions,
and increase your ability to
focus and concentrate.

The time to be
happy is now.
The place to be
happy is here.

Robert G. Ingersoll

MAGICAL MANDALAS

Mandalas are geometric designs with a circular pattern that are used for meditation, prayer and healing. They have been used for thousands of years in the Buddhist and Hindu traditions as meditational tools to clear the mind. They have also been used in many therapeutic environments to help people unearth feelings that need to be expressed. Mandalas can be used in several ways. Creating your own mandala can facilitate your personal growth; helping you become more conscious of your inner thoughts and allowing you to tap into your creativity, without the need for any artistic expertise. You can also use mandalas to enhance your meditation practice. Choose a design that appeals to you and let your mind be absorbed by the patterns and colours you see. This soothes the busy, chattering mind and allows the creative mind to break free.

GOOD NEWS

Positivity is key to a mindful
existence. Decide that from now
on you will stop spreading bad
news and only share good! Read
something positive before you go
to sleep at bedtime, and repeat
this affirmation to yourself at
regular intervals: "My thoughts
are filled with positivity and my
life is brimming with happiness."

Be happy in the
moment, that's enough.
Each moment is all
we need, not more.

Mother Teresa

PRACTISE ACCEPTANCE

Our natural tendency is to resist painful thoughts or feelings. This means we suffer two "pains" – the painful situation itself and our resistance to it! For example, you feel stressed because of an impending deadline at work and think, "I hate feeling so stressed".

The primary pain is stress about your workload. The secondary pain is feeling "I wish I wasn't so stressed".

The solution is acceptance. Let the unpleasant situation or emotion be as it is, without trying to change it or push it away.

For example, suppose you've just split up with your partner and you are feeling heartbroken. By fighting the pain ("I hate feeling like this, I need this pain to go away") you intensify your suffering. If you accept your feelings, however, you don't heap an extra layer of pain upon the pain you are already feeling – "I've just broken up with my boyfriend. It's normal to feel sad. It's OK that I feel this way."

Acceptance doesn't mean you like what is happening; it just means you accept that certain things are beyond your control. No matter what the situation, resisting the situation and feelings only magnifies the pain.

CHILDLIKE WONDER

Young children are constantly
curious. They see the
magic in everyday things
– a spider, a buttercup or
bubbles in the bath. They
teach us to stop and look
again, with amazement, at
what is in front of us. Start
viewing the world through
a child's eyes and see how
it brightens up your day!

DO LESS, NOTICE MORE

Instead of cramming as much as possible into your day, do less and do it more slowly, more fully and with more concentration. Take the time to luxuriate in whatever activity you're doing, whether you're cooking supper or chatting to a friend. You should find the experience relaxing and fulfilling when you're not rushing through tasks.

It's easy to get swept away by negative thinking and overlook what is really important. One way to be more positive in your life is to be thankful. People who have a strong sense of gratitude are happier and healthier than those who don't. It's important to take time out to appreciate all the things you usually take for granted. Be thankful for your body and the things it is capable of – hands that let you do so much, legs that take you to so many places, eyes that see the beauty in the world, and heart and lungs constantly working for your survival. This is a far healthier approach than focusing on the body parts you don't like or that are less than perfect in your opinion! Spend a little time each day reflecting on the things you're most grateful for – your health, your loved ones, your dog, the sound of laughter or a beautiful summer's day.

Drink your tea slowly
and reverently, as if it
is the axis on which the
world earth revolves.

Thích Nhất Hạnh

LIGHT A CANDLE

Light a candle and
place it on the table
before you eat. This
brings calm and peace
to a setting, alleviates
tension, and encourages
people to eat more
slowly and thoughtfully.

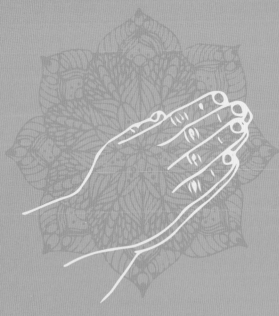

NAMASTE

The Sanskrit greeting "namaste" means "the light in me greets the light in you". On waking today, decide that you will look for the secret goodness in three people you deal with. Open your heart as you speak with them and notice how this intention affects your thoughts, and the interaction you have with them.

TAKE THREE BREATHS

Whatever your state of mind or the number of things you have to do, rest for a moment between tasks and breathe for at least three complete breaths. This will give you a much needed energy recharge to carry on with your day.

A MINDFUL
WORLD

THE SOUND OF WATER

Science has proven that "blue space" including seas, rivers and lakes can positively affect our well-being. The sight, sound, smell and feel of water calms our frazzled minds and bodies. For this reason, water is a great aid to practising mindfulness. The next time you are in a "blue space", put your worries to one side and focus instead on the physical sensations you are experiencing – the sound of crashing waves, the smell of salt in the air, the cool water against your skin or the ripples of a bubbling stream. This relaxing exercise will help you to focus on the present moment and achieve a sense of inner quietness.

YOU ARE NOT ALONE

When you find yourself caught up in a tangle of negative thoughts, place your hand on your heart. See if you can feel it beating and notice how your chest rises and falls with every breath. Think of all the heartbeats doing the same thing across the world, then move on with a renewed sense of shared experience.

SEEK TO
EXPAND YOUR

HEART

NOT YOUR
POSSESSIONS.

BIRDWATCHING

We are surrounded by birds, but how often do we stop to notice them? Place water outside for the birds – and stop to watch them wash and preen their feathers. Pay close attention to the soundtrack of birdsong that accompanies you as you go about your day.

Get up a few minutes early and give yourself time to take a gentle stroll in a quiet, calming space before heading to work. Let your mind wander as you take in the sights and sounds of nature and allow the morning air to revive you.

LOOK AT EVERYTHING AS THOUGH YOU WERE SEEING IT FOR THE FIRST TIME.

When you realize there is
nothing lacking, the whole
world belongs to you.

Lao Tzu

FOCUS ON A FLOWER

Flowers are beautiful objects, but how often do you pause to really drink in their beauty? The next time you're outside, let your gaze settle on a flower. Take in its pure, bright colour and soft, velvety petals, and inhale its delicate fragrance. See its beauty and intricacy, and place all other thoughts to one side while you marvel at the detail of this natural wonder.

TAKE NOTE OF
THE LITTLE THINGS

We're usually so caught up in our
thinking that we pay little attention
to our surroundings. This means we
often overlook interesting details.
From now on, encourage yourself
to take note of the little things, such
as what clothes a person is wearing,
which flowers are beginning to
bloom, and what colour the walls
around you are. You may be
astonished at the number of things
you have not noticed before.

COLOUR THERAPY

Look around you and focus
on the colours that you see.
Let your eyes wander as you
absorb the hues of purple
sunsets, yellow pumpkins, ruby
berries or the slate-grey sea.

STOP AND SMELL
THE ROSES

Tuning into your senses
can help you relish the
present moment. Enjoy
your sense of smell – rain-
drenched earth, freshly
baked bread, fresh fruit or
barbecue smoke. Closing
your eyes can sometimes
help to heighten
your appreciation.

the
purpose
of life
is
to
enjoy it.

ENCHANTED
FORESTS

Forests and woodlands are ideal places to go back to nature and to feel refreshed. Stand amongst the trees and soak up the peaceful atmosphere. Breathe in the forest smells: the wood's essential oils, moss and soil create magical aromas. Watch beams of light through the leaf canopy, enjoy the textures of rough bark and soft undergrowth, and look out for signs of insects and wildlife. This is something the whole family can relish, if you like – young children can run around, having make-believe adventures and discovering hiding places, while teenagers may be inspired to sit and write poetry or sketch plants and scenery. Don't forget to take a picnic to complete a memorable trip!

THINK
LESS
FEEL
MORE.

REFRESHING RAIN

If you usually avoid walking in the rain, don't! A walk in the rain can bring another dimension to your surroundings and there can be a heightened sense of smell, sound and feeling. As long as you have a warm place to dry out afterwards, it can be refreshing and revitalizing, and can wash away any blues.

URBAN BEAUTY

When walking through a bustling city turn your
eye to details – chimneys, rooftops, windows
and the abundant variety of architectural
features. Notice patterns – symmetry, circles,
spirals, parallel lines, pairs and repetition.
Allow your gaze to stay a moment in wonder
as you appreciate the intricacy and beauty
of the things humans have created.

THE SOUND OF SILENCE

Make silence a part of your life. Close your eyes and listen mindfully for one minute to all the sounds around you. For one minute, you have nothing else to do. Just listen.

Everything you
do can be done
better from a place
of relaxation.

Stephen C. Paul

You must live in
the present, launch
yourself on every wave,
find your eternity
in each moment.

Henry David Thoreau

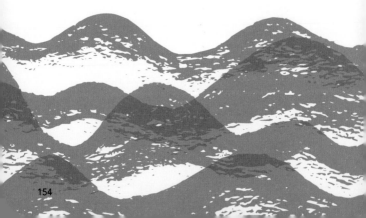

GARDEN MEDITATION

If you have your own garden,
tune in to all your senses as
you dig the soil and weed
the flowerbeds, or simply
sit and enjoy your lush,
green surroundings. If you
don't, visit a public garden
and pay full attention to
the scents, the colours and
shapes of your surroundings,
and enjoy their beauty.

MINI MOMENTS OF PEACE

Open up moments of calm throughout your day. This could be a few seconds spent in quiet stillness while the kettle boils or while your computer is switching on, or it could be as simple as taking a deep breath of crisp morning air as you leave the house.

You're only here
for a short visit.
Don't hurry,
don't worry.
And be sure to
smell the flowers
along the way.

Walter Hagen

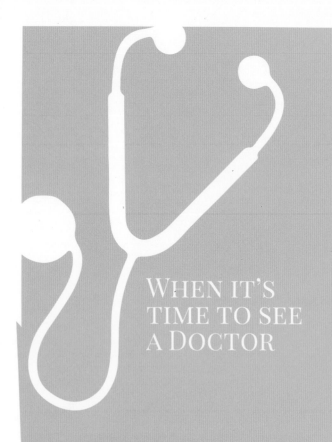

WHEN IT'S TIME TO SEE A DOCTOR